SOULFUL BLOOM

Kiandra Jeané Brooks

to Carol

because of you, my garden overflows

The flowers by my bedside are the epitome of hope deferred. The petals are rusted and I have reached the conclusion that I love me not. I need to wash.

I lost myself in a pile of colored emotions, unfolded like hands that have forgotten how to pray. I swept my true feelings under the rug, hoping they would stay. My closet is overflowing with unhung skeletons dying to resurrect. I've kept far too many worn out shirts of let down in my trunk that I can no longer fit.

I lost myself in the minus signs and was positive that happiness was no longer a factor. Silence permeated the room and I forgot the roar of my own laughter. I need to rinse. I gotta get clean. I was a fiend steady sipping dysfunction on the rocks- extra salt round love's rim-

but this time, I'm cleaning. This time, I'm clean and

I hope you see it in me to be nurtured. See enough sun in me to shine, enough growth in me to bloom...

Foundation

Femininity

Hard-hittin'
red lip poppin'
brown liner tracing
my lips to perfection-
a feminine connection.

The extension of my legs keep
pace with the Nile.
I am elongated, elevated.
I am chocolate, a hue
of coco glaze.
I grin in flirtation and the
horizon is amazed.

I am shea butter.
Lianne, Whitney, Debbie too.
I am all the rhythm,
even more of the blues.
I am steeped in the
fragrance of passion,
of peace,
of Chanel and tea on my best day,
impatience and fried chicken grease
on my worst.

But always
hard-hittin'
always
red lip poppin'

Upon Return to Miami

My dwelling place welcomes me with palm
        trees.
Intriguing me with warm sand fondling my
        short, warm toes.
Audible slingshot screams at the spades
        table with
music sped up for twice the lovin'.
I am made new upon every return.

Motherhood

Nobody tells you
that when Mama yells,
"Sit!"
molding your kinks
into a cascading carousel of twists,
she's preparing you to
conquer the twisted world
        with ease while
always looking good doing it.

Nobody tells you
that when Mama says,
"Speak up"
it's because lips glued shut don't shine
and your sparkle is worth the
world beholding.

Nobody tells you
that Mama's rants will
become your adapted life guide
to refer to in a myriad of
confusing dilemmas.

She beams
wisdom embellished
in curls.
Nobody but Mama.

For Carol

Your voice is the quilt
on which I lay my head.
Gratitude is all
I breathe.

Mama's Side, Daddy's Side

Mama's side finds my earrings to be a beauty.
Daddy's side says those hoops a lil' bougie.

On Mama's side, I hover over them all.
On Daddy's side, they all play basketball.

Mama's side craves a slice of 'Holy' cake.
Daddy's side slaps juicy ribs on the plate.

Both sides bring hearty jokes and good times.
Mama's and Daddy's side, forever both mine.

Me, Myself and I

Being an only child
is getting to know
yourself very well.
Us three, we get along
just fine.

House of Brooks

When I was a little girl,
I hated my last name.
Not because the double O
was tough to jump through,
nor because people would
teasingly say Books instead-
shoot, I loved to read anyway.
It wasn't the fact that it starts with a B.
See, that was a perk.
I was always
almost first
for everything in school.
Truthfully, I earned it.

But my last name was far from home.
It didn't look like the world around me.
My last name was nestled in a place
that required me to take a flight,
or at least days and nights
on a bus to get there
and greet it.

It didn't dance around the house with me
in socks and oversized tees.
It didn't float into my school for
graduations,
concerts,
and conferences.
It didn't match the tune
my mother's name sang,

the Brown
of her
and granddad
and cousin
and
everyone else
in between.

When I was a little girl,
I hated my last name,
not realizing it would be the
last paternal piece,
a hidden treasure
I would keep of a man
so distant
yet, close in laughter
and love.
This last name is
all I've got.

Brooks is all I've got and
never has a name
welcomed me
home more.

Mississippi Memories

Our memories are fond-
the familiar chiseled whiff
of cigarette bud,
calls long overdue,
the rough grasp,
the savory cuisine,
the blurt of your words a sharp edge
slick enough to cut a chicken clean.

I remember it all.

The Grandest

They are bedazzled beauties,
faith cloaked in fashion.
These ladies of mine hold a power
gentle as hair follicles, freshly pressed,
louder than the turquoise
brooches on their dresses.

These misses are a hit,
voices lifted in harmony to Nazarine
and beyond.
These ladies are the bomb-
tick, tick
      Baby Boomers teaching lessons like:

> *Clean panties are a woman's superpower.*
> *Never leave the house without snack money.*
> *Keep a secret or two for you*
>   *live.*

I worship the ground they've constructed
with their hands, all polished fine and fair.
My grandmother's sisters hold me as their own,
twice more for all the
times she never could.

Gloria's Deviled Eggs

She is goodness.
A savory aura of spice,
a paprika to your life.
She is petite with a kick that invites you in
with a mixture of warmth and lessons.
Her deviled eggs just as memorable...

Reserved

Nicknames are bestowed
as a rite of passage,
used only by
the village;
a privilege.

Ode to Pop, 2012

People knew him as Shagg, or Mr. Brown.
To my cousins and I, he was plain
old "Pop" when we were around.
No words could describe the loss
of such a great man
But I know that this is all a part of
God's glorious plan.

I'll miss our good times, like sneaking
out to Burger King,
buying the whole menu-
well except the healthy things.
And the times he never interrupted
the arguments Mama and I went through,
Because he himself was afraid that
she would fuss at him too.

I could never forget sitting on the porch
having our story times.
Watching him burst into various songs
at the drop of a dime.
Picking him up randomly, having fun
wherever we were.
Driving all around the city,
him calling me his "little chauffeur."

No matter where we traveled
across the town,
Everyone knew of kind hearted
Mr. James Brown.

Goodness ran through his body
from his head down to his ankles.
We are beyond blessed to now have
such an amazing guardian angel.

Hothead

I'm a girl that cries when angry.
My tears come to a gradual boil.
Silent, sporadic, seething
like water in a pot, awaiting
fresh eggs or
fresh braids
(ready to be dipped).
Approach me with caution,
with care.
Wrap your fingers,
wrap your heart,
wrap your mind around the idea
that it is simply best
you wait 'til I cool.

305

Let's set up the dominoes and charades,
hop in line for Krispy Kreme glazed
jooking at the MLK parades.
This is home.

That Betty Wright
making you feel all right,
no sign of going home in sight
and this is home.

Conch salad from the spot,
weaves slayed at the shop,
damn, it's just too hot.
This is my home.

Families growing older,
the kids no longer sober,
the crimes are getting bolder.
We're coming home.

The soil can only do the job of the soil. It can't make the sun beam brighter, nor the rain fall lighter.

Devastation

Re: Missing Girl

I once knew a girl
named Joy.
She crafted miracles
and swallowed sorrow whole.

It has been months
since she was last seen.

You both left
around the same time.
One voluntarily,

the other against
her own will.

Inebriation

My wardrobe is drenched in sin,
tipsy off the ways of the world.

Anxiety

Nothing
halts
my breath

quite
like this
leaving

my airways
clenched
in fear

always
tip-toeing
to my
desires

always
hesitant about
every
step prior.

I am uncertainty
wrapped
in
discomfort.

Sweet Tooth

I'm convinced
you were put on my shelf
for a reason.
A glimpse of sweet temptation,
a price tag that rang up
to one of a kind every time.

You are the Now and Later
I sneak before a meal,
the Kool-Aid cousin always
puts her foot in.
Without you, my breath
reeks of sadness
and ain't shit sweet about it.

But you're too much for this
diet of mine.
I cut unhealthy foods long ago
and I haven't craved you

in days...

Happy Hour (Last Call)

How could something so sweet
as the view of a bee perched on
a honeysuckle laboring for nectar,
turn as sour as an amaretto
waiting for its lover
to return for another sip?

Loneliness

The last time I had good sex,
tomorrow slipped into our sight.
Your skin glazed over mine like frosting
our tongues so tangled,
we almost forgot how to breathe.
Your erection rectified my
feelings of loneliness,
only for me to come
to the conclusion that
you still weren't straight up
and I was still empty.

The Vow

Oh, how I yearn to hold you,
to hold us in time and space,
to hold me up from the fast pace.

I hold you close,
hoping you hold these too.
I love you
but to have and to hold
I no longer hold onto.

Sea Sick

If these walls could talk,
        they'd whisper the names of
                every snake that has
                        slithered through
                        my grass, leaving behind
                        damaged fruit,
                they would spill all the
        unfathomable truths,
        explaining in length
the nights of me sailing
        away
        wailing...

Her Unborn

inspired by Frieda and the Miscarriage

The nightingale sulks
in sorrow,
perched over
my unborn,
never to clasp
golden jewels.
Never to sow seeds,
my blood fresh
as pigs slaughtered
hours before.
I now know pain
and loneliness
intertwined.

Cadence

The impulsive
cadence of my heart
      leave
             stay
      leave
             stay,
somehow perfectly
echoed the symphony that
was our disaster.

Resemblance

Pulling leather with
buttery hands
seems impossible.

That was the epitome
of loving you.

Homegoing Waltz

There is something about us and funerals.
The precision of
how we sway in grief,
all in step
1-2-3,
      rest-in-peace,
our peace has been uprooted.
We are trees grown tired from gloom,
we coordinate in color,
an ensemble of subdued tones,
belting out classical goodbyes.
Yet we keep rhythm,
a synchronized army of broken soldiers marching in
stumbling,
longing-
we've done this before.
We sit, we gather,
knowing we will soon waltz again.

Black Boy Somewhere in America

Hello Sir, how can I help you today?
I couldn't sleep last night in fear
that today would be my last day
but that's nothing new here.

I'm mentally in system overload,
the system's killings are over toll
and the senseless killings are far untold.
Don't tell me how to feel,
you damn sure don't know.

I'm standing, I'm marching,
I'm all confused
because powers are misused and
hashtags won't do
and the next one
and the next,
I don't know who.

Love hard, pray harder
stay informed, get smarter,
be strong, no
stronger
but what do I do if
I want to live longer?

Listen here man, what do you want today?
Don't tell us how to feel or what to say.
The wretched thing is,

this is nothing new, you've just
never had to worry as much as we do.

Mama raised me right so, I don't
need much from you.
All I ask is that
I have my right
to remain alive—

That'll do.

They Told Me

They told me to pick a color
and crimson
filled my head,
the way blood floods the streets.
They told me to pick a color
and my stomach turned an un-royal blue,
a jump rope haven knotted and punched.
They told me to pick a color
and a hundred times too many my eyes have seen
chestnut, mocha, mahogany
skin, sunken into the cracks
of sidewalks lifeless.

They told me to pick a color
and sirens blurred my vision,
viridescent thoughts heard my cry.
They told me to pick a color.
Black.
They told me to pick a color
Black.

Uptown

If there's one thing I know holds true,
every place wasn't made for you.
Holding you back from whiskey
and snare sets
'cause the way you're dressed.
Forever reminding you
that to them, you're
"black at best"

But night, at its best,
is black.
Chestnuts best when roasted,
bread savory once toasted.
So, save your dollars
for the next
time you're out
spending it somewhere
other than Uptown.

A Black Girl's Send Off, June '11

Red and blue pounds against my eyelids
at flashing pace.

She just wanted the perfect send off.

The scent of prejudice filling the air,
mama's store-bought chicken,
the perfect accent.

It comforts me.
Friends gliding past in horror,
entering my house,
tears gliding past my cheeks,
entering my mouth,
a salty delicacy for the evening.

She just wanted the perfect send off.

My wrists,
clasped
then hands
sprawled,
yearning for a fighting chance.
I'd just been given the chance
to attend my dream school.
The backyard overflowing with loved ones,
because that's what we do.
But a policeman and a black girl's
happiness don't mix.

She just wanted the perfect send off.

Years later, and
that scent of prejudice still lingers.
My screams for help
still ring in my ear.

Random Notes to Whom It May No Longer Concern

One,
I still mourn at the thought of you.
Your hugs were always
the perfect bowl of soup in the cold.
Our inside jokes burst through
crowds, forever leaving us joyfully aching.

> Two,
> on my long days I go into
> a long daze, thinking of all
> the ways you broke me.

Three,
what used to be my favorite novel
has become a tattered book
of nostalgia,
never to be read again.

> Four,
> I shot
> unhappiness and lime regularly.
> You're to blame.

Five,
I am sure you're reading this
unaware that this is about you.
You always whisked oblivion and
nonchalance masterfully.

Whimsical

I heard stories of masks
worn by people past.
The fairytale pictures,
worshipped in class,
never mentioned
a mask like yours.

Valentine's Day

I've been struck by Cupid's
bow three times now.
Each time,
the head much sharper,
letting go much harder.

Cardiac Talk

It is fascinating
how the heart pumps
vigorously from your time
in the womb until the time
it speaks wailing a cry of no more.
Shutting down and creating
a domino effect of loved
ones never to be held again.

Maybe it's not so fascinating after all.

Maybe, Maybe Not

When fire extinguishes in a relationship,
rifted lovers often search for the
errors of their ways.

Maybe space was too much.
Maybe space wasn't enough.
Maybe you had more to offer
        than you showed.
Maybe we rushed.
Maybe we went too slow.
Maybe we'll never know.

Maybe I took too long to show
what my love is really about.
Maybe you moved on too fast
and never heard my love out.

Just maybe…

Not So Safe Sex

They say be safe
and wrap it up…
But what good is it
if the heart is
forever left
unprotected?

Splash

I died to be good
to you. Every day
I hopped on
your mood swings,
chains as rusty as
our conversations
we now pour in rivers
of nothingness.

100 Piece Puzzle

We fit.
Like children, we forced
two puzzle pieces
to connect.
Too lazy to match the picture
on the box, so we made our own.
I wasn't the corner to your side
but whether the blame is
our naivety
or creativity
damn, we fit.

Rainbows

Our love was a rainbow:
always more visible
after the storms,
infinitely beautiful
and never long-lasting.

Undefeated Demon Slayer

I battle demons in silence.
Fighting with my bare heart,
my hands quaking in fear
that my truths
may be uncased.
My voice withholding screams,
ashamed that someone might
discover my secrets.
I have yet to be found out.

When words cut as deep as the rocks settled beneath your soles,
take that same blade and carve a masterpiece

Restoration

Amen

The best grace
was giving thanks
to God for a smile
like yours.

Long Before

You were art long before
the name Picasso could tumble
with ease off your tongue.
Long before your brain could fathom
yellow plus magenta equals red,
long before you and your first
heartbreak exchanged glances,
long before the verses were written
and mountains were chiseled whole.

Your season is awaiting
your arrival.
It will embrace you with
open arms long before
you come to be ready.

But get ready,
stay ready,
long before.

OOTD

When you wake in the morning
how do you dress
your insecurities?

Are they plastered on your outerwear,
nestled in embroidery,
worn proudly like mascara
both voluminous and bold?

Do you tuck them in your blouse,
only to strut them around the house
or do you slick them into
your baby hairs, hoping no one
ever notices the imperfect blend?

Possibly, behind those ears
that have heard countless times how
incapable,
unlovable,
you are
or

are your anxious thoughts
the culprits of the pucker in your socks
that you protest as fashion,
when in reality they've become the
ankle weights that
hinder and
break you?

It will never be a perfect love story. Love at first sight will always be a stranger. Finances will see-saw uncomfortably. The rally of screams, bouncing off the walls, will become the pattern that compliments this tone of love best. But this companionship will be full. Bellies swelled from the satiation this love brings. Affection and attraction will attack slowly, infectious, contagious. It will never be a perfect love story. It will forever be a story of love.

U-Train

If you were ever
to take a ride
on my train of thoughts,
you would find your name
splattered across every seat,
a washable paint that somehow
managed to stain
indefinitely.

Solid

I want to wake up
next to a lover,
willing to put me back
to a tranquil sleep.

A lover refusing to
waver when the tides
become unbearable.

A lover whose chest
is velcro-manufactured
'cause I can never seem
to detach to start the day.

Bonded by Bonnets

The spring of curls at 7 a.m
taught us at an early age the
importance of bouncing back.
Each bonnet a warm
stadium of preservation
hovering over our heads
like beloved guardian angels.
Oh, the tales they've heard.
Oh, the tails they herd.

The kinks of our coils
hold stories unknown
that can be traced back to woman
who had no concern of blending in,
giving us all that early-morning-hair-frizz
type of attitude that not even the
thickest gel could control.

We pledge allegiance to our nightly routine,
for it is in this satin we thrive-
twist outs, pineapples, braids
all deserving of a hiding place.

Never forget to
tuck it all in, girl.
Your ends deserve,
like your roots,
your hair,
your life.

All needing to be protected
and preserved.

We are forever bonded by bonnets
you and I.
From your roots
to the end.

Practice Makes Perfect

My therapist is my
track coach,
training me up to run
each and every hurdle

and after every
glorious victory,

bringing me back
to train.
For there is still
work to be done
and races to be won.

Long Lost Sista

Oh, my black girl
act just like me.
Your smile as wide,
feet too.
Our laughs reminiscent of
summer tea,
      sweet tea.
           Sweetie, you're art like me,
stories swirled in loc'd twirls,
dipped in the finest of paints.
We embody the sketch
of greatness,
of royalty.

My Black girl,
though your tongue be laced
in the finest of H-Town threads,
mine Miami-bred,
we forever speak the same language.
Our eyes never before laid eyes
but our spirits have danced a duet.
We've crafted a bond
as tight as old school shoelaces,
double-knotted,
           double-knotted.

Hey sista', soul sista'
let the world behold sista'

Respect to the hands, the years of labor, to the voices cat-scratched a jazzy rasp, crying out for justice. To the words that have lived on to tell stories to generations for generations. To the ways the blues sing a black woman's life song; her fingers interwoven around her pen- her only saving grace and safe space in America. So, we recite, we respect, and we pay homage.

Awaken

May the buses of life
refuse to rush through
puddles of burdens,
leaving you soaked
in the middle of
nowhere
this time around.

May your heart stay
warm in the
toughest of winters.

May you awaken
with a vengeance
that glows and yells,
I'm here.

Transformations

Time isn't watching
hands of a clock stretch.
Rather a feeling,
a heart's transformation
from broken
to half-way whole.

Is and Isn't

It is not just bubbles in a bath tub,
massages and face-masked-manis.
It is not just a splurge to the store
for the superfluous that won't come in handy.

It's beyond the Mute and the Do Not Disturb
buttons we seem to retreat to.
It's more than a date all by yourself,
even though we all have to eat, true.

It's in the way you speak up for yourself
and the boundaries you set everywhere.
It is the strength of your No's
and your therapy glow.
Now that
        is truly self-care.

Beauty Shop Talk: A Haiku

Sitting in her chair
wise words make me feel brand new
hairstyle just as fresh

Escaping the Cape

I know generations of women that
have worn capes for years, passing it
down a traditional armor,
swaddling and saving the same ones
our capes were created to free ourselves from.

Dearest Girlfriends

We are a clique of ladies.
Click clacked in our high heels,
sometimes sneaks,
all various physiques,
exchanging all the feels.
From Waiting to Exhale moments,
keeping it real,
to the breeze of our candid
brunch conversations,
encouragement overflowing
with the libations.

Plant Mom Lesson #701

My plant
shows me every day
the power of knowing
when to cut things
off to bring in
something that may not
look different,
but it is for sure much
more
alive.

You once snatched everything in life- but life from me. I'm here for my things.

Liberation

You Did That

Why do you celebrate
yourself in whispers,
as if you are uncertain that
the praise is due?

Just as sure as the check's
submitted every month on the first,
don't be late
giving yourself the applause
the little girl inside you
has long awaited
and deserved.

Creation

You can't tell me God
doesn't create amazing things.
I've beheld the
rise and set
of sun,
the fall and
rise
of women.

Roar

I am a lion
no mane
        more beautiful
no man
        more powerful

ferocious and fierce
I am woman

Duality

I am not a one-dimensional bot,
only programmed to showcase
minimal features.
I am a muse,
all of me in 3D,
fluent in softness and power,
alike.

Insomnia

Legs interlocked,
clock ticking-tock,
Big spoon, little spoon.
Temperature raising
         gimme some room
and this is how we sleep.

Cold feet sending alerts.
No undergarments, just a shirt.
Brush it up and tie me down,
bonnet on, don't make a frown.
And this is how we sleep.

Blossoming bosom, your hands cup
passion ignites and I erupt.
And this why we get no sleep.

To Be Whole Again

A lot of men have given up on me.
A lot of men have given up on loving me.
Truthfully,
I messed up.
I picked and chose when I
wanted to show love,
give love,
be love
and worse,
I was wanting them to make me whole
when they were all half
the man they should be.
Luckily,
I never gave up on me.
I never gave up on loving me and
truthfully,
now that they're gone,
I'm more of the woman
I'm supposed to be.

Tables Turned

Kickball was a game
of being chosen by others,
sometimes last even.
Life has become a game
of choosing myself first,
each and every time.
Even when I am lost,
I have won.

Vision Board Party 2021: A Note

Audacious black girl,
it's time you thrive.
Take fear head on
with God by your side.

Put your anxiety at ease,
perfect all the poses,
limit negativity,
inhale the media in doses.

Believe in creativity
'cause it truly gets no better.
Stay humble and sport
your smarts like a sweater.

Here's to love that soothes
to a job that brings you smiles.
to activism, laughter, and joy
that keeps you for a while.

Thrive, audacious
black girl.

Spelling Bee

Spell divine.
　　　May I have the definition?
of, from, or like God; excellent
　　　May you use it in a sentence?
Even without makeup, her beauty is divine.
　　　Any alternative pronunciations?
Black girl magic.

"5,6,7,8"

They ask me why I dance,
why I can't seem to sit still,
why the beat fills my spine with
euphoria every time,
not knowing trauma
sits in these hips.
Every body roll, an attempt to
rid myself of the past.

These movements never
betrayed me.
Can't you see, the dance
in these hips
saved me?

Snow Angels

When summer turns to
fall and fall to winter,
I find comfort in sitting
by the window,
peeking, as the children
play for the day.
Curiosity oozing from the
stitches in their mittens,
I peek in admiration,
          in relief
that on this day, Black bodies will

flutter freely in the snow
rather than lay stone cold
in the road.
That happiness will be
tucked in a coat,
rather a dream choked
and held captive in a bag
of untouched possibilities.

This icy swish of flailing arms
will leave imprints that are memorable.
That are as cool as ice
cream on a cone,
two scoops after the football game.
If only for a day,
they are noticed.
They are mighty.

These Black bodies are delicate.

I yell from the house,
through the frost bordered pane.
Leave your mark.
Knowing they can't hear me,
hoping all the more my words,
like their coats,
keep their fiery energy
ignited within.

Eviction Notice

My body was never yours to keep,
you were simply a tenant
just for a lease.
I let you accessorize, settle in
feel like home in it.
Knowing all the while
I'd never sign off on
this long-term commitment.

Now here you are violating.
Let's be clear:
You must pay.
The easiest resolve?
Pack it up,
move away.
I'm not sure where you'll land next.
It's not for me to decide.
I just know of
someone better,
who's worth
living on the inside.

A-mazing

It amazes me
how you navigated
the maze in me.

Your hands,
firm with support,
calloused from the labor
you put in loving me
consistently.

You are my favorite jewelry.
The statement piece my
life's been missing,
forever worn and adored.

Quarantine Lovin'

It has been seven months,
two weeks, three days
and counting
conjoined in the living
room with another.
May we never forget
the time well spent
becoming each
other's favorite
book to read
time and time again.

Dedications

I'm not a fan of dedications, but if I were
a page with set margins would not be enough.
You make me color outside the lines.
With you, the limit is non-existent.
Oh, your gaze,
         your waves.
I'd make my words jump off the page
and sing for you.
Even curate a self-made playlist or two,
reminding you of everything you
mean to me.

If I was a fan of dedications…

Renewal

The rattlesnake never molts in shame.
She relinquishes her skin
with pleasure,
for she knows the ways of her past
have become brittle,
useless baggage
that slows her down.

She has outgrown her brokenness and
must restore herself back to worthy
so, she sheds
to reveal something much more radiant.
A candy bar unveiled,
she is the golden ticket.
For a moment, she is unshielded,
exposed
but in exchange for pristine newness,
she consents.

On this day,
spot her,
become her, and
may you too
be reborn.

Plucked

Confidence was a gift bestowed upon me
at the rightful age of ready falling
into my lap unexpectedly,
with a menstrual and
budding breasts
to tag along.

But she wasn't always there.

She sat in a tree for years,
until I deemed myself worthy
of plucking her for myself.

Illusions

On any given day,
my body shape shifts
becoming my worst enemy.
A villain.

My scars,
my stretch marks,
my cellulite,
all viciously
screaming
to be noticed.

The mirror, an accomplice,
using my reflection to distract
and inflict pain
but my mind
is the hero,
arriving in the knick
of time to remind
me how this body of mine
is forever a temple,

a sacred ground of worship
and praise.

Garden of Women

I've mingled with magnolias,
their presence as gentle as
perfect plush pillows,
enduring each and every
transition with poise.

I know a sunflower or two.
Women who
are forever adorned,
always there beaming
external rays of light.

How lucky of me to
dance with dandelions,
youthful in all their ways
light on their feet,
they blow me away.

I am swarmed by roses
classic ladies, refined,
romantic. Could swoon any
being from the Pacific to Atlantic.

I once met a peony,
she prayed for me.
Took us both to God and
I've been stuck ever since.

I am a seed, sprouted from a
garden of women that vary
vibrantly- some savory, others sweet
backs strong with nutrients,
the backbone, the nucleus.

And together, we create
a masterful garden,
forever in bloom.

We are together, forever, in bloom.

Leap of Faith

She's trembling,
inching to
the edge.
Staring in admiration at her
dreams across the way,
hoping they stand still,
hoping they receive her
with arms wide open.
She takes it all in,
she takes faith
and flies

and
soars.

*And then the day came when I reached deep down in my purse,
beyond the faded receipts and wilted mints
and found peace.*

I know the feeling
of losing it all.
I've watched life
snatch my joy,
but today,
I know my soul
and my soul is well.
The road
hasn't been painless
but I know it all
makes for a more

Soulful Bloom.

Acknowledgements

Having a desire as a young Black girl to write a book and actually writing it are two very different things. As of late, I've learned that one is much easier than the other. Yet, here we are.

Mom, thank you for always providing guidance and candid realities. You were my first teacher of self-love and independence. I am appreciative of you and everything you have taught me. My love for reading and words has fallen directly from your tree. I value your love and support, always.

A very special thank you to Abraham for being the most supportive accountability partner. There is no one like you. Thank you for showing up for me even in the moments I was too doubtful to show up for myself. You make me feel unstoppable. I'm sure you're happy that the end of this book finally means a good night's rest (for now). I love you.

To my amazing family and village. I am the sum of each of you, and I am grateful for you all being there every step of the way. To my sister Raquel for every random uplifting call and text. Your spirit is genuine and treasured. To Daddy and Pop, I miss you both dearly. I know you two would be proud.

To my close circle of friends who have supported me along this tedious journey and have inspired me creatively to keep going despite the odds, I thank you. Tiffany, Christina, Samiya, Ciera, Ojette, Iyanna, Erika, Marcus (who didn't even know this was a thing, but his talks and work ethic have been pivotal to this process), and countless others.

To the Hardworking Kappa Epsilon Chapter of Delta Sigma Theta Sorority, Incorporated that has taught me the importance of detailed planning and quality execution. To my amazing line sisters that hold me accountable to speak my truth and do it big always. Your sisterhood and support are forever cherished.

To my amazing editor, VanessaDreams, for her feedback and encouraging words. To my cover designer, E.R.Canedo, for bringing my vision to life in an unmatched way.

Who knows if she will ever see this but thank you to Ms.Audrey Silverman, my ninth-grade English teacher, who told me how great my writing was (even when Mom felt like it still needed work). I will never forget your encouraging words and feedback that have helped propel me forward as a poet. I hope this book one day falls into your hands.

Sharing my words in a book that will last and last has been the most frightening yet joyous, liberating thing ever. I finally have something I can call my own.

To God.

To you.

Kiandra Jeané Brooks is a writer, educator, and performing artist, born and raised in Miami, FL. With a B.A. in English from Florida State University and an M.S. in Education from Southern Methodist University, her love for words and Arts advocacy runs deep. *Soulful Bloom* is Kiandra's debut poetry collection.

Made in the USA
Las Vegas, NV
27 June 2021